Essay Writing Made Easy

for Everyone Who Hates to Write Essays

a step-by-step process to create
organized and meaningful essays your teachers want

Shannon Michal Dow

𝒫 Phosphene Publishing Company
Houston, TX

Essay Writing Made Easy
©2012 by Shannon Michal Dow
ISBN-13: 978-0615731773 (Phosphene Publishing Company)
ISBN-10: 0615731775

Published by
Phosphene Publishing Company
Houston, Texas, USA
phosphenepublishing.com

Dedicated to my brother, Chris, for his eternal support.

Also authored or co-authored by Shannon Michal Dow

Non-fiction

Writing the Award-Winning Play

Plays

Killing Dante

Dark Passages

The Moorlark

Table of Contents

Introduction

Your teacher assigns you a five-paragraph or a five- or ten-page essay. Honestly, what is your gut reaction? Anxiety? Doubt? Dread? Uncertainty? Confusion? Hopelessness? Horror? If you're anything like my high school students were, it's at least one or maybe all of these. How will you come up with an essay topic? How will you figure out what to put in your paragraphs? How can you possibly fill up five *whole* paragraphs (let alone, *five whole pages*)? And *why* do essay grades count so much toward your overall grade?

Why Do You Need to Know How to Write an Essay Anyway?

I hear this question quite often. *"What's up with all this focus on essay writing?"* you might ask. *"I'm want to be a [insert job that you think doesn't require writing here], not an author!"* I'm going to take a moment to try and briefly convince you why it's in your best interest to be a competent writer.

Number One: Being able to put together a logical and meaningful written document is something a lot of current jobs require.

Number Two: Colleges and universities want their students to be able to engage in what's called "critical thinking." In other words, they don't want students who just memorize facts and understand what they read; they want students who can apply, analyze, evaluate, and synthesize what they read and know. Being able to write an essay demonstrates these abilities. (Why else do you think colleges and universities ask for essays on your application and the SAT and ACT have an essay section?)

Number Three: Most careers now and into the future require a potential employee (that would be you) to have *at least* a two-year degree; many require a four-year degree. The best-paying jobs will want their employees to have that "critical thinking" thing. They want their employees to be able to think on the job.

Number Four: The more years you go to school beyond high school, the more money you will earn. Over your lifetime, this could add up to hundreds of thousands of dollars. Let me repeat that: *over your lifetime, this could add up to hundreds of thousands of dollars.* Now you might be someone for whom money has no meaning. If you are, I applaud your strength of character. However, you might be someone who sees money as a means to a goal, in particular, financial security. If you are, then you should aim for getting into college and earning a degree in one of the top ten careers that will pretty much guarantee you a job when you graduate.

Why You Need an Easy but Detailed Guide

You may find that because of your panic at the idea of writing an essay, you do several things that undermine the end result. Do you put off writing the essay until the day (or night) before it's due? Do you find yourself adding really long quotes or enlarging your font size to 13 or spreading out your line spacing to triple space or increasing your margins (hoping your teacher won't notice) just to make the essay fit the required length? Do you end up retelling the plot? Do your paragraphs flounder like a fish on the sand, with no place to go? Is your conclusion nearly identical to your introduction? Do you write something that follows this format: "My essay will be about . . . In this story there are (first point), (second point), and (third point) . . . First of all . . . Next . . . Finally . . . In conclusion (or) As you can see, I have shown (first point), (second point), (third point)." (You know what I'm talking about!) Are you tempted to just cut and paste from the Internet, which, in case you didn't know already, is plagiarism and can get you kicked out of college? If you answer yes to even half of these questions, then this guide is for you. It will help you through the sticking points; prevent formulaic, boring writing; and enable you to approach the essay with creative ideas.

What's Wrong with How Essay Writing Is Taught?

First of all, it's not your fault that the essay writing assignment causes so many unpleasant thoughts and anxieties. Most students are taught a very boring way to write essays all the way through middle school. What is this style? It goes something like this: Introduction: I will write about [assigned topic]. I believe [assigned topic] because of Reason One, Reason Two, and Reason Three. Body Paragraph topic sentences: Reason One, Reason Two, Reason Three. Conclusion: a complete restatement of the Introduction.

Why is essay writing taught this way? In the elementary grades, it's an easy way to introduce the essay style. However, many teachers tend to keep insisting upon this basic style all the way through 8th grade instead of building upon it. When I assigned my 9th grade students their first essay, requiring at least a five-sentence introduction, a thesis, body paragraphs that actually analyzed and didn't just summarize, and a conclusion that was completely different from the introduction, they freaked. It was so alien to what they'd been required to do in previous years. However, after attacking the essay as a step-by-step process that takes place over time (and not in one all-night session), they not only ended up with wonderful five page essays, they were also extremely proud of what they accomplished and how unfrightening the whole process was once they had experienced it.

It's not completely the teachers' fault either. In Connecticut, the state education department requires that all public school students take Connecticut Master Tests (CMTs) in English and Math up through 8th grade. Schools "fail" or "pass" based on these test scores, and new regulations would require teachers' pay be tied to student scores on these tests. No wonder teachers teach to the test, which, for the CMTs, means teaching the good old persuasive essay and only the persuasive essay. Students even are informed they can make up "facts" to prove their argument, the total opposite kind of thinking required of essays in high school and college.

So what's wrong with this basic (if boring) kind of essay writing? It's not too relevant once you're past 8th grade. In high school and college, you are expected to analyze, evaluate, or synthesize and provide *actual* proof from you source material. This demonstrates the higher level kind of thinking your high school and college teachers and future bosses will expect. If you approach the writing required of you in school and your careers as if it were like the typical 8th grade essay, you may be viewed as lazy, unmotivated, or incompetent, at the most crucial times of your life – the ones that will most likely determine your future success.

Why Is *This* Guide the Best One for You?

Now that we've established that you do need to be able to write in a logical, analytical, cohesive way, why is this guide the best one for you? Some essay writing guides are meant for instructors who teach essay writing. They either are only very basic with the expectation that the teacher will fill in the blanks, or else they are too complex, using terminology that may make most students' heads spin. Some guides are supposedly geared for the student, but they only outline the basic purposes of each paragraph, leaving it up to you to figure out how exactly to fill up those paragraphs. There are some guides that might go a little further by explaining what a thesis is and informing you to use transitional sentences. But even these don't actually tell you *how* to come up with a thesis and develop it. They don't give you step-by-step help you in a detailed and less agonizing way to come up with a great thesis, write logical paragraphs, and end up with solid essay.

How This Essay Guide Is Different

So just how is this essay writing guide different from any other essay guide you can buy in book form or view for free on-line? It's meant for you – the one who actually has to write the essay. And it's meant to make your essay writing as painless as possible. That's not to say you won't have to do the work, but at least the process won't be as confusing or as exasperating. And the more you follow this format for all of your essays, the easier writing each essay will become. In this book, I've presented the same method I used with great success with my students in the class room. It's a process that chunks each step of the essay process so that writing the essay won't seem as overwhelming and impossible. You may never learn to love writing essays, but you will learn to write a good, solid essay. Who knows – you might even end up with a great one.

How to Think About Essay Writing

Think of the process of writing an essay as if you were blazing a trail to the top of a mountain. When you first begin the hike, there isn't even a trail. Your hike may be difficult because you have to figure out which is the best way to reach your mountaintop. You have to cut through the woods to make a trail that leads you in the most logical way. Since you've walked through the woods once before, you come across familiar guide posts where, one by one, you leave behind a trail marker. Along the way, you come across different guide posts, but if you stray from the trail you are blazing, you might get lost. You may never reach the top of the mountain, or you may reach it only after sloshing through a swamp or hacking through dense undergrowth, arriving tired and confused. But if you stay on your path, you will reach your goal.

The woods in this case are the novel. The goal you have at the beginning to reach the top of the mountain is your thesis statement. The trail you make is the sum of the evidence you use to prove your thesis to reach your goal: quotes or actions of characters that reveal their motivations or beliefs; quotes that reveal the author's theme; the author's use of language, voice, and tone. The hiking guide you end up creating is your essay. Before your "hiker" starts out, she looks at a map you've given her. She finds the beginning trail marker you have designated and starts out on the path that will lead to the top of the mountain. She arrives at the top only because of the trail markings you've left along the way to guide her. Once at the top, she has a sense of satisfaction; she may even see something she's never seen before. She only has this experience because of the trail blazing you did beforehand. Just as the guide logically and meaningfully leads to the top of a mountain, your essay logically and meaningfully leads to its purpose – a thesis that no longer is hypothetical, but has now been proven true and may even reveal a deeper, unique, or more profound truth than had ever been considered before.

Important Notes before You Start

If you are writing formal essays, as analytical, argumentative, and persuasive essays are, you need to be aware of a few rules beforehand. Following these rules to begin with will make it easier when you proofread your essay because they will be one less thing you will have to correct.

Rules for Formal Essays

Rule #1: Never use "I", "we", "us", "mine", "my", "our", or in any way refer to you. For instance, do not use "this reader" to refer to yourself.

Rule #2: Do not use "you", "your", or in any way refer to the reader. Don't use second person unless it's part of a quote.

Rule #3: Don't use slang, colloquialisms, or informal language of any kind.

Rule #4: Do not use contractions unless they appear in a quote from the book. Instead, use both words that make up a contraction (do not, will not, etc.).

Rule #5: Use present tense throughout your essay whenever you write about literature. The only times you use past tense when writing about literature is when you are using a quote that is in past tense or when you are discussing one part of the novel and need to refer back to an earlier part.

Rule #6: The first time you mention the name of the author, give his or her full name. After that, refer to the author by last name only. **ex.: first mention:** Charles Dickens wrote *Great Expectations.* **all other mentions:** Dickens portrays Pip as a snob. The only exception to this is when writing in APA style. When writing in APA style, never use the author's first name.

Rule #7: When writing *about a particular work* or works, always mention the title in the introduction. When writing *about a topic that you have researched*, you only need to mention the work or author plus proper citation when you are discussing a point that uses the work as evidence.

Rule #7: Be sure to use the style your teacher requires: MLA (usually high school and undergraduate) or APA (graduate and sometimes undergraduate).

Rule #8: Provide appropriate citations.

Tone and Voice

Just because an essay is a formal kind of writing doesn't mean it has to be bland with no personality (although some kinds of graduate writing, such as the literature review, require no personality). Tone is a literary term that describes an author's attitude toward his/her subject matter or audience. You should have an attitude toward both. If you're trying to argue your thesis, it would be logical to use a tone of respect toward your audience, especially if the intended reader is your teacher! As for your attitude toward your subject matter, such as an author's theme, you can adopt a different tone: serious, humorous, sarcastic, satirical, annoyed, shocked, offended, etc.

In addition to tone, voice is particularly important for narrative essays. You want to give the readers a sense of who you are in a narrative essay. In this kind of essay, you can use language in ways that are not permitted in formal essays. You can use contractions, colloquialisms (sayings that are common to a particular area of a country), slang, and dialect. In fact, you should use them in order to give your narrative essay an interesting story-like quality.

Different Types of Essays

Usually your teacher will assign a specific topic for your essay or give you a limited choice of topics. You will need to decide what type of thesis statement will work best for the assigned topic and kind of essay. Most often for high school, you will be writing a persuasive or an analytical essay. High schools are also moving toward requiring more argumentative essays, which are also common in college, along with analytical essays. Occasionally, you might be asked to write a narrative essay. Expository essays, which require you to explain a step-by-step process, are used mostly in classes such as science, math, culinary, physical education, and business.

This guide will focus solely on the analytical, persuasive, and argumentative essays.

Analytical essays require you to break down your topic into parts that you then must analyze and evaluate part by part. You prove your interpretation of each part by using evidence from your source book(s). As a whole, all of the parts add up to proving your thesis. For example, you might analyze the author's use of language and how it is used to create mood; the changing of a character from the beginning to the end of the story and what the author is showing through this change; or how actions, dia logue, and narration point to a particular theme. These essays are most common with analyzing fiction.

Persuasive essays are the ones most often required in high school. These require you to argue a claim and provide evidence from your source materials for that claim. This relies on providing facts from other sources and not analyzing a particular source itself. These are the essays where you are to take a stand one way or the other. For example: argue pro or con on the topic of should marijuana be decriminalized; argue pro or con on the topic of should texting while driving be illegal. In a persuasive essay, you take only one side and prove why you think that side is the correct one.

Argumentative essays require you to make a claim about the topic that is open to debate. These essays are often about non-fiction topics. In order to prove your claim, you must provide proof by using evidence from your source book(s). Your claim could be an opinion, a cause-and-effect, an interpretation, or an evaluation. You also show evidence for the other side of the argument. You can acknowledge a piece of evidence, but they you must discredit or minimize the importance of it. For instance, there might have been 500 sightings of the Loch

Ness Monster over the past five years, which seems like a lot. However, if it turns out the same two people were the only witnesses the seeming importance of the 500 sightings is now minimized. (By the way, I made this up just to show an example.) While persuasive and argumentative essays may seem very similar, there is a major difference. Like a persuasive essay, in an argumentative essay you present a claim and then provide evidence to support the claim. However, unlike a persuasive essay, you also present opposing evidence and acknowledge, discredit, or minimize the importance of it.

Expository essays require you to explain how something works or is put together. Think of it like a recipe that explains how to bake a German Chocolate Cake or a car manual that explains how to repair a 1968 Volkswagen Beetle. Like any essay, it must have logical flow and be somewhat interesting to read.

Narrative essays require you to essentially write a story that is true. In this case, you are the narrator. It has all of the components of a story: plot, including setting and other exposition, rising action, climax, and falling action; characters; conflict; and theme. You may be asked to write a narrative essay based on an experience from your own life, or you may be asked to write one from the point of view of a character in a novel. The thesis statement tells the reader right away what the story is about.

The Thesis Statement
The Guiding Purpose of Your Essay

 Always write your thesis first.

The thesis statement gives you a goal and a focus as you write your paper. It also tells the reader what the focus of your paper is. A thesis statement is usually only one sentence, especially for papers less than 10 pages.

 A thesis should concern a theme, idea, concept, conclusion, or principle that is a major factor in the book.

When brainstorming about your thesis statement, remember that it should be about a concept that you can infer from (conclude from) the novel. This conclusion must be based on details and quotes from the book that refer to this concept. It should *not* be merely a fact or an event from the book.

Although you could prove that in the novel *To Kill a Mockingbird*, Jem Finch sees prejudice in action at the trial of Tom Robinson, a good thesis statement would *not* be: *Jem witnesses prejudice at the trial*. Why isn't it a good thesis statement if you can easily prove it? It doesn't *need* to be proved because it's already a fact. There is nothing about this thesis that required you to draw a conclusion based on a number of sources (details and quotes) from the book.

However, you can look at the abstract concept of "prejudice" and write a thesis statement that has to do with the unfairness of prejudice. That means you should come up with a thesis you can really discuss with some confidence.

A thesis should be provable.

I might tell you that the theme for George Orwell's *Animal Farm* is "the good guys always win." My paper's thesis could be "In a world of sadness, the good guys always win." But I would be wrong. Nowhere in Orwell's novel is there evidence to substantiate this thesis. Because there is no evidence, I wouldn't be able to prove this thesis. Your thesis must be backed up by solid evidence from the book.

Authors write their books with their own perceptions of the world in mind. If the book is well written, one or more of these perceptions will be the basis of a theme. Similarly, a well written book will use literary devices and techniques to help convey those perceptions. The theme of a well-written book isn't like the solution to a bad murder mystery where vital clues are withheld until the end or where the murderer makes an appearance only in the last chapter. If it were, it would be impossible to figure out what the author is trying to say to the reader. A careful author will sprinkle "clues" throughout the story, leading the reader along a purposeful path. When this path ends, the reader should feel that the clues actually did amount to something meaningful.

You, as the reader (or as the interpreter of the clues), are, then like the detective in a murder mystery who pieces together the solution to the case. As the writer of your essay, you have to show and explain to your readers this evidence and the conclusions you've come to because of the evidence. In this stage, you become more like the prosecuting attorney who lays out to the jury the proof he's gathered that led him to a particular conclusion. A good prosecutor needs to present this evidence in a logical, clear, and provable manner. But you do need the evidence.

Evidence comes in the form of details from the book; something a character says; the way the narrator describes a scene; the scenes and actions the author chooses to emphasize; repetition; the double meanings of words, just to name a few. In order to be real evidence, it must be repeated more than once or twice. For instance, if it rains one day in a novel, that may, at most, be a means to set the mood of that day. But if it rains, and a bath tub overflows, and a boy drowns in a pool, and a girl's tears drop onto her hand – all that *water* is evidence of *something*. The author doesn't accidentally put in all that wetness; it is purposeful; it is saying to the reader, "Hey! Look at this! Notice this! Figure out what it means!" This is the kind of evidence that will prove your thesis.

> A thesis should be reasonable,
> credible, and provable.

Let's go back to the *Animal Farm* example. If you don't know the novella, in a nutshell, *Animal Farm* is about the revolt on a farm of badly treated animals against their human masters. Once the greedy and cruel humans are driven off the farm, the animals begin to work the farm together, declaring that all animals are equal. By the end of the novella, the pigs have enslaved, starved and murdered other animals, becoming even more greedy and cruel than the humans ever were. It would, therefore, not be reasonable or believable for a thesis for *Animal Farm* to be: "In a world of sadness, the good guys always win." While this is a rather obvious example, you still need to consider if all aspects of your thesis are reasonable or believable. If not, you need to rework it *before* you finish your first draft. Believe me, once you have put all of the effort into writing that first draft, you are not going to want to start over because half of your thesis isn't believable.

> A thesis should have
> a deeper meaning.

"There is a lot of prejudice in *To Kill a Mockingbird*." This is not a thesis with a deeper meaning. "The realization that the world is filled with evils such as prejudice forces one to grow up." This type of thesis makes your readers (and you) really think about the topic.

 A thesis statement should not be too simple or too narrow.

Take the time to come up with a complex thesis statement. But doesn't complex mean difficult? Not really. What if you had to write a five-page essay that had this thesis statement: *Writing five page essays is difficult.* Would you actually have enough information to write an entire essay on this topic? Probably not. More complex thesis statements actually make it *easier* for you to write a solid essay because there will be more parts you need to prove, and you will have more information with which to prove them. These parts will become the topics of each paragraph. Make sure these parts logically make sense together.

EX.: *To Kill a Mockingbird:*

> **too simple:** There is a lot of prejudice in *To Kill a Mockingbird.*
>
> **more complex:** The prejudice in *To Kill a Mockingbird* leads to misunderstanding people.
>
> **most complex:** Maturity results from the recognition and acceptance that injustices and cruelty are real aspects of the adult world.
>
> **too narrow:** People are prejudiced against Boo Radley.

 A thesis statement should not be too complex or too broad.

You don't want to end up with a thesis that is impossible to prove within the page limit. A thesis that tries to intertwine too many subjects (even if the author *has* intertwined them) takes a lot of detailed outlining and you would probably end up with at least a 20-page paper. It would be too complex for most essays required at the high school and undergraduate level. Remember, you don't have to write about *everything* or provide *all* of the evidence to write an effective essay.

A thesis with a topic that covers a wide area in a vague way will also get you into trouble. You will probably not be able to write enough or with any kind of depth.

EX.: *Romeo and Juliet:*

too complex: Impulsive behavior can lead both to love as well as to destruction, especially when those who are involved will not act rationally, some because of youthful inexperience and others because of past grievances; however, the act of both love and destruction can lead to the resolution of past grievances.

too broad: Shakespeare's view of young love is both delightful and tragic.

Different Types of Thesis Statements

There are some specific types of thesis statements that you are most likely going to have to develop.

Thematic Thesis Statements are basically the same thing as stating what the theme of a particular work is. A theme is what the author is trying to say he thinks is true about certain emotions (love, jealousy, hate, fear, etc.); about certain ideas (loyalty, war, heroism, desire for power, prejudice, etc.); about how the world is (groups fight each other for control, families stick together, people follow traditions, etc.). A theme is always expressed in a sentence. This is best for an analytical thesis.

 You do *not* have to agree with what the author is expressing through the theme. It is the author's point of view, not yours that you are trying to explain.

Character Thesis Statements: You may be asked to write about how the protagonist changes from the beginning to the end of a story; how the antagonist creates conflict; how a minor character is important to the plot or theme or conflict; how two characters compare and contrast in regard to morals.

Language Thesis Statements: You may be asked to write about how the author uses different types of language (similes, metaphors, imagery, tone, etc.) to produce a certain effect in the writing. You may be asked to write about how the author uses words to create mood. You may be asked to analyze the author's tone. (Explain how it's sarcastic, humorous, or satirical.) An essay that attempts to do any of these is more of an upper-level or college level assignment. This is best for an analytical essay if you have to examine the novel only. If you are looking at other critics' views of the work, then it would be an argumentative essay. Possible for narrative if you're writing about the dialect or slang in a certain part of the country from your point of view.

Compare and Contrast Thesis Statements: You will be asked to find the similarities and the differences between two or more characters, books, settings, etc. Although this kind of thesis and essay might seem simple, many students make several mistakes. Best for argumentative, analytical, or narrative theses.

- Don't forget to contrast. Most do fine finding the similarities, but forget to find the differences.

- Don't make trivial comparisons or contrasts. One character may have blue eyes and the other brown, but does it make sense to put that in your essay? Unless the similarity or difference is *meaningful*, don't mention it.

- It is also important to find a way to relate the similarities and differences and to come to a conclusion. Find meaningful examples that somehow connect to each other. For instance, two characters might have the same kind of childhood, but end up quite differently. Compare their childhoods, contrast their lives, and come up with a reason *why* they ended up so differently.

- Don't put in *all* of the similarities and *all* of the differences. If you do, your paper will be crammed with a list of comparisons and contrasts that may overwhelm the reader. You also may find it difficult to relate all of the material in a meaningful way (unless you plan to write a 25-page essay). Again, find meaningful examples that somehow connect to each other.

Creating Your Thesis Statement

 Before typing a single word of your essay, ask yourself these questions. Take down notes as you think about the answers.

1. What is the topic your teacher has assigned? Your thesis will, of course, have to be about this topic in some way.

2. How is this topic a part of the work or works you must write about? Or, for a non-fiction thesis, how is this topic a part of your world or society's world or the whole world? Think about this and jot down or type up a few notes.

3. Which characters deal with this topic the most? If you're writing about a non-fiction topic, what kinds of people deal with this topic the most? Again, think about this and write down or type up some notes.

4. How does this topic affect those characters (or, in the case of non-fiction, real people), their lives, their personalities, their actions, their futures? You might want to think about how the characters change (or don't change) because of this topic becoming a part of their lives. Again, jot down or type up some notes.

5. What message is the author trying to get across to the reader by writing about this topic?

6. Can you find a lot of evidence by way of details and quotes from the story (or other articles or real events) that will support what you've noticed and that inter-relate in some way?

7. Does your thesis statement mention the overall topic? Have you have determined what the work is (or works are) saying about that topic?

   EX.: *To Kill a Mockingbird:*

   a. **possible topics** – prejudice; an adolescent maturing into adulthood; understanding people for who they are, not what they seem; justice and injustice.

   b. **What might be true about these topics in the novel?** – prejudice is destructive and unfair; maturing involves learning that the world is unfair; one needs to consider life from another person's point of view in order to understand them; the world is not always just.

   c. **Which characters are most affected?** – Jem, Tom Robinson, Boo Radley

   d. **How are these characters affected?** – Jem: realizes prejudice exists in his town; realizes the court system isn't always fair; realizes that prejudice against a person result in that person's false imprisonment or death; these realizations make Jem upset. Tom Robinson: seems to try and "stay in his place" as dictated by white society in order to get as fair a trial as possible; seems to already know he'll be found guilty; runs for the fence because he's given up hope. Boo Radley: People gossip about him, calling him some kind of monster; he is forced away from society when he's a teen, and remains a recluse because he has no contact with the outside world; sees Jem as the boy he used to be, which results in his following Jem and eventually saving his life.

e. **author's messages:** Prejudice leads to destructive acts; prejudice is passed down through generations; prejudice leads to false impressions; the adult world is not always just; when a child understands that the world is not always just, he/she begins to become an adult.

f. **evidence:** There is a substantial amount of evidence you could use to discuss any of the author's messages.

g. **thesis:** You can see how prejudice, understanding people, maturing, and justice are important to this novel and can be inter-related. So you could come up with a more complex thesis:

— By understanding the destructive nature of prejudice, Jem learns that the world is not fair and must grow up in order to deal with it.

— Understanding people by considering events and attitudes from their view-points is part of being mature.

 Take the time now to write your thesis statement.

Make sure it –
- ✓ is interesting and thoughtful
- ✓ can be provable
- ✓ is complex enough
- ✓ addresses the assignment

The Complete Essay Guide

A step-by-step detailed guide to writing an essay is presented over the next pages. This includes a detailed approach to writing your Introduction, Body Paragraphs, and Conclusion. However, you shouldn't write the Introduction first, the Body Paragraphs second, and the Conclusion, even though this may seem to be the logical approach. Instead, follow these steps to help you better keep your essay organized, logical, and unified. You can use the **Essay Outline Template** at the end of this book for this process.

The Process:

1. Write the thesis first.
2. Write the reasons why you believe this thesis is true.
3. Come up with at least three topic sentences that incorporate these reasons.
4. Assign the reasons from Step 2 to the topic sentences.
5. Order your topic sentences so that they logically build upon each other.
6. Come up with at least three pieces of evidence that prove the reasons in you have assigned to the topic sentences.
7. Explain how the evidence is proof of the reason.
8. Write the Introduction.
9. Flesh out the Body Paragraphs.
10. Write the Conclusion.

 Think of composing your entire essay in the same way you compose a single body paragraph.

Entire Essay	Body Paragraph
thesis statement	topic sentence
paragraphs that each prove part of your thesis statement	sentences in the paragraph that provides evidence and your analysis of the evidence that proves your topic sentence
conclusion – what you've proved in the essay	concluding sentence – what you've proved in the paragraph

I. Introduction

Think of the Introduction as an inverted pyramid where a general idea leads to more a specific explanation about the work you are analyzing and then finally leads to the specific thesis statement. If you are analyzing a single work or comparing two works, always mention the title of the book(s) and the author(s) in the Introduction. If you are using several sources, then your in-text citations (following either MLA or APA format) is sufficient.

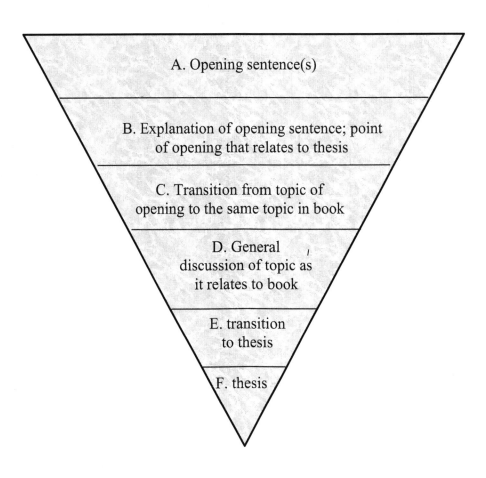

A. The First Sentence

The first sentence is a "grabber," something that gets the reader's interest. It doesn't have to be specifically about the book, movie, or whatever you are writing about. It *must* have some meaningful connection to your thesis. Here are some of the ways you can write your first sentence:

1. **Use a quote that relates to your thesis and that you can develop a rational connection to your thesis.** You could do this two ways –

   a. If your thesis dealt with prejudice, you could look up quotes about prejudice and find the best one that relates to your thesis. Search for your topic and quotes (prejudice quotes).

   b. You could find a quote in the book, story, etc. (a quote is anything that is in the source material, not just something said by a character.)

 Be sure to give attribution to the quote.

Always mention who said the quote or where you got the quote from.

      EX.: "Judgments prevent us from seeing the good that lies beyond appearances," notes Wayne W. Dyer, author of *Ten Secrets for Success and Inner Peace.*

        OR

      EX.: "'If there's just one kind of folks, why can't they get along with each other? If they're all alike, why do they go out of their way to despise each other?'" Jem Finch wonders when he is faced with the consequences of prejudice in *To Kill a Mockingbird.*

 Jem's spoken quote is in single quotations, while the whole quote is in double quotations (because it is quoted from the book). Whenever you quote a person from your source material, you need to use this format.

2. **Use an anecdote (short story) that has some kind of meaning that relates to your thesis.** This is effective if you begin the story in the Introduction and conclude it in the

Conclusion. This gives your essay a circular form and, thus, feels complete to the reader.

> **EX.:** When John Smith, an African American, was a young boy in South Carolina, he often heard cruel and hateful comments about his skin color.

 In your Conclusion, you can relate how the adult John Smith's experiences of prejudice have or have not changed.

3. **Use an allusion** (a reference to something in history, mythology, well-known literary works, movies, plays, poems, the Bible).

EX.: In ancient Greece, Odysseus's life was turned upside down, preventing him from returning home, because the gods could control his life and destiny.

EX.: Hitler's German army was on the verge of taking all of Europe when Japan attacked Pearl Harbor, a move that brought the United States into World War II and sealed both the fate of the Japanese as well as the fate of Hitler's Nazi party.

In the first example, your paper doesn't have to have anything to do with Odysseus or ancient Greece. But your paper must deal with the idea of fate. In the second example, the paper doesn't have to be about WWII, but it does need to be about a situation in which someone who is about to succeed causes their own destruction.

4. **Begin with a question.**

 Your question must be very thought-provoking in order to be effective or this opening will seem really weak.

Don't ask questions like –
   * Do heroes exist today?
   * Is there prejudice in the world?

Instead, ask what are known as "open-ended" questions. These are questions that don't have obvious "yes" or "no" answers.

✓ What does it take to be a hero?

✓ How has it come about that some people view those of other races as inferior?

If you choose this kind of opening statement, make sure your essay answers the question you have posed.

5. State an interesting or unusual fact or opinion. The fact or opinion must be extremely relevant to your thesis. The opinion can be yours, but is more convincing if it is that of a well-known person or group.

6. Explain background information. By using this alone, you take the risk of writing a boring opener. To spice it up, try to present the information by using technique **7**.

7. Paint a scene. Use description to set the scene of the times of, place of, or an event relating to your book material. You can even quote or paraphrase from the book itself. This kind of opening can be combined with all of the openers already mentioned or it can be an important aspect of the novel (or whatever) you are writing about. Make sure the scene you describe is very interesting in terms of what is happening and very important to establishing your thesis.

B. The Next Two Sentences

The next two (or three) sentences should explain your opener and, in a general way, discuss the topic of the thesis. *Don't* write "This quote means . . ." or "In my essay I will write about . . ." or "The topic of this essay is . . ." or anything like that. Instead, write about the meaning or purpose, or your interpretation, explanation, or meaningful thoughts about the first sentence. After all, you came up with this opening for a reason. What about it made you feel it relates to your thesis (and the novel)?

EX.: opener: *What does it take to be a hero?*

next sentence: *In today's American society, a firefighter saving a person from a burning building is sometimes considered no more heroic than a drug dealer who has made a lot of money. The concept of what it takes to be a hero is a reflection of the society in which that hero is born.*

EX.: opener: *In ancient Greece, Odysseus's life was turned upside down by angry gods who prevented him from returning home because they could control his life and destiny.* **Next sentence:** *Ancient Greeks believed the gods predetermined each of their fates, and these fates* *could never be altered, no matter what they did. However, in the English Victorian society of Great Expectations, fate was determined by one's own actions.*

 The second and third sentences should be making an observation or point that connects your opener to the book you are writing about.

Because your opener may not specifically be about the book you are writing about, you need draw your reader's attention to what you want your reader to get from it. What idea expressed in the opener connects to your book and to your thesis topic.

The second sentence, specifically, should: –

✓ add more depth to your opener.

✓ connect to the third sentence.

The third sentence, specifically, should –

✓ connect the observation or point you're making to the next sentence.

C. The Next Three to Five Sentences

These sentences are specifically about the work or topic you're writing about. You'll connect the observation or point you have started to develop in the first three (or four sentences) directly to your thesis. Continuing the examples from above, you might develop them like this:

EX.: opener: *What does it take to be a hero?*

next two sentences: *In today's American society, a firefighter saving a person from a burning building is sometimes considered no more heroic than a drug dealer who has made a lot of money. The concept of what it takes to be a hero is a reflection of the society in which that hero is born.*

next three--five sentences: *Odysseus was born into a society that valued extraordinary abilities, such as super human strength, enormous courage, vast intelligence, quick thinking, and great cunning. These may seem to be obvious traits of a hero. However, Odysseus's society also valued other traits they associated with the hero – loyalty, honesty, hospitality, love of family, and the ability to express the human emotions of grief, love. They also despised greediness, pettiness, and lust for power, none of which would be considered heroic characteristics. A man* *who combines all of the traits honored by ancient Greek society was considered to be above all normal men.*

EX.: opener: *In ancient Greece, Odysseus's life was turned upside down by angry gods who prevented him from returning home because they could control his life and destiny.*

next two sentences: *Ancient Greeks believed the gods predetermined each of their fates, and these fates could never be altered, no matter what they did. Thousands of years later, in the English Victorian society of* Great Expectations, *fate was determined not by the gods, but by one's own actions.*

next three--five sentences: *Charles Dickens's tale is of a young boy, Pip, who, in his journey to manhood, makes several choices that affect him nearly as harshly as the gods' choices affected Odysseus. He nearly loses the love of those who love him the most and even becomes despicable to himself. Yet, his life is not the result of inescapable fate predetermined by some outside force, but comes from a path of his own choosing. Just as he had the power to make choices that lead him to a life that makes him unhappy, he is also able to make choices that ultimately redeem him.*

See how I expanded, explained, and detailed this part so that I ended up with a good number of sentences that are still important to my topic?

It's better to explain or detail too much in a first draft than too little. It's easier to cut or combine sentences than to think up new ones.

D. Your Final Two Sentences

These sentences connect the whole Introduction's purpose to your thesis statement. Remember that inverted pyramid Introduction graphic? You have gone from a general example, expression, allusion that deals with your thesis topic to the thesis itself. Here are possible last two sentences, including thesis statements, for the previous examples.

EX.: (next to last sentence) *He was an epic hero – larger than life because he was the role model for the ideal man.*

Thesis: (last sentence) *Through his actions and emotions, Odysseus proves himself to be such a man -- larger than life – an epic hero worthy of the Greeks' admiration.*

EX.: (next to last sentence) *He has the power to change his life.*

Thesis (last sentence): *Pip's maturity come from his realization that his choices have led to unhappy consequences coupled with his desire to try and make amends for these consequences.*

 Always mention the title and author of the book in your Introduction, then, try not to keep repeating them throughout your essay.

There are several ways to mention the author and title. Here are a few:

- In the novel *Great Expectations* by Charles Dickens . . .
- Dickens shows in *Great Expectations* how . . .
- In the novel *Great Expectations* Pip is . . . (another sentence) Dickens demonstrates . . .

 Take the time now to write your Introduction.

Make sure it --

    ✓ Has an interesting opening sentence
    ✓ Gives the reason this first sentence is meaningful to your thesis
    ✓ Connects the opening to the work(s) you are writing about
    ✓ Connects the work to the thesis
    ✓ Ends with the thesis

II. Body Paragraphs

Body paragraphs, taken as a whole, prove your thesis. Here is the logic:

- ➤ In the beginning, your thesis is an unproven statement. It is your job to prove it.

- ➤ Each paragraph has a topic sentence. Each topic sentence is a specific point you believe to be true about your thesis. If you can prove your topic sentence is true, you will have proven part of your thesis. Once all topic sentences have been proven, you have proved your thesis.

- ➤ In each paragraph, you will give reasons, evidence for those reasons, and explanations of the evidence to convince the reader that your topic sentence is true. If this evidence does prove your topic sentence, your topic sentence is now true. Since your topic sentence is now true, part of your thesis is now true.

- ➤ Once all topic sentences are proven to be true, you have proven your entire thesis.

- ➤ Once your thesis is proven, it becomes a fact, a truth. It no longer is the unproven statement it was in your Introduction.

A Word on Summarizing

Don't do it! Believe me, your teacher doesn't want you to retell the plot of the book, she wants you to *analyze* the book. It's true that you will need to provide *some* context for the evidence you're providing, but how do you do this if you aren't supposed to summarize? First of all, consider your audience. If you're writing for you teacher, which in most cases you will be, you can assume she knows the plot pretty well already. Therefore, you can introduce evidence from the story *briefly*, usually in a sentence or less.

> **EX.:** *After Pip comes into his "great expectations,"* (brief summary), *he turns into a snob.* **NOTE:** You don't have to explain when he got his money, or who the lawyer is, or his reaction *unless it is crucial to your main argument.*

> **EX.:** *Napoleon drives Snowball off of the farm and then takes over completely.* (brief summary)

The important thing to remember is that no matter what you use to explain the context, it must be *brief* and *only* set up the *meaningful* context of your evidence. One way to prevent you from resorting to summarizing is to get rid of the idea that your body paragraphs and the sentences within your body paragraphs have to be in the same chronological order as the plot. Since your topic sentences are meant to prove conceptual points and not plot points, you never have to present the evidence in the same order as it appears in the book.

Once you free yourself of this idea, two things will happen.

1. You can concentrate more fully on the *reasons* you believe your thesis is true, and

2. You will be less likely to just summarize the plot for the bulk of your essay.

A. The Topic Sentence

Your first or second sentence in a paragraph is usually your topic sentence. This should be as interesting and nearly as complex as your thesis statement. Just as the thesis statement guides you in the writing of your essay, each topic sentence gives you a focus for your paragraph.

 Never use a quote as your topic sentence.

The topic sentence serves three purposes:

1. It takes part of the thesis that needs to be proved and clearly expresses what you intend to prove.

2. It tells the reader, as well as you, the writer, what the paragraph is going to be about.

3. It provides you with a focus for what you will (and will not) include in this paragraph.

 Come up with all of your topic sentences after you have written your thesis statement. This will give you overall guidance and structure.

What Should Paragraphs Be About?

Look at your thesis statement. This is what you've told your readers you are going to write about and prove. Include *only* evidence, details, and explanations in your body paragraphs that are necessary to achieve this goal.

Underline each part of your thesis that you will need to prove. Look at what you've

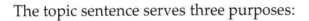

Through (1) <u>his actions and emotions,</u> (2) <u>Odysseus proves</u> he is such a man – <u>larger than life</u> – an (3) <u>epic hero worthy of the Greeks' admiration</u>.

underlined. Each of these will be the topic of a paragraph. In this example, you will need to write paragraphs that prove:

(3) What the Greeks thought were qualities of an epic hero.

(2, 1) How Odysseus's actions demonstrate he is "larger than life" (and thus, he fits the qualities of an epic hero).

(1, 3) How Odysseus's emotions demonstrate he has normal human characteristics (lust, boastfulness, pride), but mostly represent ideal emotional traits (loyalty, determination, honesty).

You could easily write a paragraph about each topic. If you prove all of these topics, you have proven your thesis.

 Never use a plot detail as a topic sentence. Some poor topic sentences seem like they are making a statement, but really they are just plot points.

EX.: *Jem goes to Calpurnia's church where there are other African Americans.* (It's hard to write an entire paragraph proving this, because it is already a fact. It is possible that his going to the church might be used as *evidence*, but not as a topic sentence.)

EX.: *After Tom Robinson's trial, Jem learns that people in Maycomb are prejudiced.* (While this is true, and does relate to the topic of prejudice that might be the subject of a thesis, it's not really making an important statement. As in the previous example, this is a fact. This should be used as to prove Jem's new awareness of the prejudice in Maycomb.)

Decide what would be the logical order. Which of them do you have to prove first, second, third, etc.? Think of yourself as a police detective or a prosecuting attorney trying to prove that a specific person committed a crime. You have pieces of evidence, but you must assemble them together in a logical way so that it shows just how this person is responsible. Sometimes it is necessary first to prove important information in one paragraph so that this information can be used as a fact for another paragraph. Logically, the paragraph upon which others build their case needs to be first.

B. Proof and Explanation

After your topic sentence, the point of your next five to eight sentences is for you to --

- ✓ give a reason why you believe your topic sentence is true.
- ✓ provide evidence for that reason from the text (quotes, details, actions, and the author's use of language).
- ✓ explain how your evidence is proof of your reason.

| Every sentence in a paragraph is geared toward proving the topic sentence. |

For each topic sentence you will need to provide reasons why it is true. Follow this pattern:

1. State a reason or belief that, if true, will prove all or part of your topic sentence.

2. Provide evidence of that assumption. If this assumption is the only one you are making for this paragraph, you need to provide at least three pieces of evidence. If you are making another closely related assumption, provide at least three pieces of evidence for the entire paragraph.

 Every paragraph must contain more of your own writing than words quoted from the text. You shouldn't use too many quotes.

3. Explain why this evidence proves the assumption.

4. Provide a transition to your next piece of evidence or to your next assumption.

5. If all of your textual details, evidence, explanations, defense that the evidence does, in fact, support your assumption, you can conclude that your assumption is true. Since this assumption is now no longer an assumption, but a proven truth, your topic sentence is now true.

C. The Last Sentence (or two)

Your last sentence or two serve two purposes –

1. reemphasizes the point you were trying to make in your paragraph. In this way, it draws a conclusion based on what you've proven in your paragraph.

2. transitions to the next paragraph in a logical way.

 Never end a paragraph with a quote.

What Else Should Be in Your Body Paragraphs?

✓ **transitions** – so that your argument flows smoothly and is logical. If one sentence doesn't logically follow another, you will have to move to where it is logical, provide a transitional sentence so that it does make sense. (*see* Transitions, *p. 46.*)

✓ **great vocabulary** – When you write your first draft, don't worry so much about using sophisticated vocabulary. Go ahead and write, "The consequences of Pip's actions were bad," realizing that "bad" is not a very precise word. Later, use a Thesaurus (in book form or on-line) to find the perfect word. Don't just plug in the first word you see. Make sure it really has the meaning you intend. (Yeah, you might have to actually look it up!) So, for

"bad" you could use instead, depending on what "bad" is supposed to mean in your context, – "corrupt, wicked, cruel, hideous, defective, rotten, nasty, incorrect, doubtful, harmful, questionable, spoiled, unfavorable, fearful, uneasy, sulky, regretful, heartbreaking, unpleasant, unattractive," just to name a few. There is quite a difference between "The consequences of Pip's actions were cruel" and "The consequences of Pip's actions were defective." Make sure you write what you mean.

✓ **evidence** -- This is what you need from the book to prove your reasons, which will prove your topic sentence, and, thus, to prove part of your thesis. Your evidence must be to-the-point and effective. Evidence comes in several forms: a quote from a character that demonstrates your point; a quote from the narrator that demonstrates your point; a quote from the author (not to be confused with the narrator) to demonstrate your point; a detail from the book that demonstrates your point; a paraphrase of an action or conversation that demonstrates your point; a quote from an outside source (if permissible) that demonstrates your point. (All must be properly cited.) Notice that I keep saying, "that demonstrates your point." That's because this whole paragraph is meant to prove something specific and needs evidence that specifically proves it.

What Should NOT Be in Your Body Paragraphs?

✗ Evidence that doesn't belong. Never put in evidence that does not help to prove your topic sentence. This will cause the paragraph to lose focus and, perhaps, logic. Keep referring back to your paragraph's topic sentence to make sure your evidence helps to prove it. A good sign that you've added something that belongs in another paragraph is when you write, "Also . . ." Sometimes that "also" can be developed into an entire new paragraph.

✗ A statement or observation you don't support with evidence from the book.

 Something may be true in the novel, but still not belong in your paragraph.

 Take the time now to write your topic and sentences, then reasons and evidence, then the each full body paragraph.

Make sure each paragraph --
  ✓ Has topic sentence that helps to prove your thesis
  ✓ Has reasons why this topic sentence is true
  ✓ Provides evidence from the text(s) to support the reasons
  ✓ Explains how the evidence supports the reasons
  ✓ Concludes with a sentence that transitions from the point made in this paragraph to the topic of the next paragraph

III. Conclusion

Think of the Conclusion as a pyramid. Unlike the Introduction's inverted pyramid, Conclusion's pyramid goes from specific to more general. It begins with the apex (or point), which restates the thesis, and moves to the wider portion, which has broader and more generalized information. In the Conclusion, the restatement of the thesis leads to a more generalized discussion about how this thesis affects the novel's meaning, to an even more generalized statement about what has been learned because of discovering the truth of the thesis.

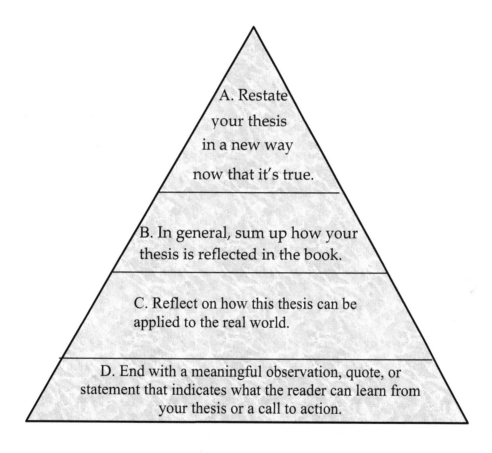

A. Restate your thesis in a new way now that it's true.

B. In general, sum up how your thesis is reflected in the book.

C. Reflect on how this thesis can be applied to the real world.

D. End with a meaningful observation, quote, or statement that indicates what the reader can learn from your thesis or a call to action.

A Conclusion is not a restatement of your Introduction. It's not simply a copy of your thesis and the topic sentences of your body paragraphs. It's much more and should be as unique as your Introduction. At this point, you have proven your thesis to be true. It is no longer speculation on your part, but is now a fact because of all of the evidence you've provided. The Conclusion should let the reader know in a brief way what you have proven, why this is important, and what meaningful insight the reader can take away after reading your paper.

 Never include in a Conclusion any new evidence or observations that you haven't already mentioned in your paper. You can refer to evidence and observations that you have discussed in your paper, but only do this generally.

A. First Sentence

Restate your thesis as if it is now a proven fact. Don't just put in the same thesis sentence in your Introduction. Now that you've proven your thesis to be true, think of it in a deeper way. You will want to express the heart of your thesis statement.

> **EX.:** from *To Kill a Mockingbird*
>
> **thesis statement in Introduction:** *Maturity results from the recognition and acceptance that injustices and cruelty are real aspects of the adult world.*
>
> **re-expression of thesis statement for Conclusion:** *Children often are unaware of the injustices and cruelties that exist in the world; but when they do become aware they often struggle to understand the adult world they are about to become a part of.*

B. Next Several Sentences

More generally, discuss how this new truth impacts the meaning or understanding of the novel or work if fiction or society, human behavior, policy, laws, etc. if your essay concerns non-fiction sources.

EX.: from *To Kill a Mockingbird* (a continuation from the previous example)

For Jem, the shocking realization that the prejudices in Maycomb can lead to the conviction and eventual death of an innocent man is his first step into the adult world.

C. Next Several Sentences

Now discuss how this new truth enhances your understanding of the world.

EX.: *The existence of prejudice seems to be something that has existed since man began. It makes one group of people feel superior to another without any real justification.*

D. Last Sentence

What should this truth mean to your reader? You can use a meaningful or shocking quote, a thoughtful observation or comment. What should the reader take away after reading your essay? How is your essay meant to make the reader think about human nature, society, the world, war, gun control, etc.? You might ask for a call to action – something the reader can do to make a change in the situation. You might make the reader question his beliefs about a topic. You might just emphasize the point of your essay by ending with something ironic, satirical, humorous, or serious.

Take the time now to write your Conclusion.

Make sure it --
   ✓ Restates the thesis as something that has been proven true
   ✓ Generally points out how it relates to the work(s)
   ✓ Does not add any new evidence from the text(s)
   ✓ Connects the thesis to the real world in some way
   ✓ Ends with a meaningful message/observation

The Little Extras

Once you have your essay written you can sigh and pat yourself on the back. You've done a lot of hard work. But you're not done yet! Put your essay aside for a day or two, then go back and read it with fresh eyes. Here are the things you'll want to work on.

The Title of Your Essay

 Give your essay a really great title that hints to the reader what the essay will be about.

Don't title your essay: "Essay," or "Name of Book Essay," or "Name of topic Essay." Be clever and creative. Mention the title of the book(s) in your essay if you are writing an analytical essay or a comparative essay. You can develop great titles in any of the following ways.

EX.: The Effects of Prejudice on Coming of Age in *To Kill a Mockingbird.*

- **a tiny key bit of a quote that is in your paper --**
  Climbing Inside Another Person's Skin in To Kill a Mockingbird

- **a play on words or symbolism that suggests your topic –**
  Killing the Mockingbird
  or
  Judgment in a Small Southern Town

- **a repetition of some key phrase you might use in your essay –**
  Awareness of the Adult World in To Kill a Mockingbird

- **a very brief restatement of the main point of your thesis.**
  Through the Eyes of Children: The Repercussions of Injustice and Prejudice in To Kill a Mockingbird

Transitions

Transitions suggest a particular relationship between one idea and the next. They help the reader connect the dots – to follow the same logic you had. Too often writers *think* they've said and explained what they mean, but in reality, have left out the connections. They either stick in quotes without first giving the reason the quote is supposed to illustrate or else don't connect the quote to an explanation of how this is an illustration of the reason. The result is confusion for the reader.

How to Transition Between Points

Never assume that your readers know what thought process got you to make your points. Think about it – you had to take time to piece things together in a logical way. Your readers need you to do the same thing for them. Guide your readers through the same thought process you had when you came up with your points and evidence. It's much better to give them too much instead of not enough guidance. This will often require an entire transitional sentence.

 Transitional words and phrases often occur at the beginning of a sentence and are set off with a comma in formal essays. The Internet has many lists of transitional words and phrases and when to use them.

There are three basic ways to provide transitions between ideas:

1. using transitional expressions, such as: furthermore, pointing out the idea that, instead, in a complete reversal, suggesting, etc. These expressions should show the relationship between the ideas expressed in the sentences. There are many lists of transitional phrases online.

2. repeating key words and phrases – This ties your ideas together because of the repetition. Be sure to use repetition in a thoughtful way and not because you can't think of a better phrase or word.

3. using pronoun references – If your character's name is Joe Bloe, you can refer to him as "he" if it's clear that he is the person you're writing about. If he's a doctor who graduated from Yale and who is married to Martha, you can also refer to him as "the doctor," "Martha's husband," or "the Yale graduate."

List of Transitions

addition	also, again, as well as, besides, coupled with, furthermore, in addition, likewise, moreover, similarly
clarify	furthermore, further, in other words, put another way
consequence	accordingly, as a result, consequently, for this reason, for this purpose, hence, otherwise, so then, subsequently, therefore, thus, thereupon, wherefore
compare	similarly, in the same way, likewise, just as
contrast	in (by) contrast, by the same token, conversely, instead, likewise, on one hand, on the other hand, on the contrary, rather, yet, but, however, still, nevertheless, in contrast,
emphasis	above all, chiefly, with attention to, especially, particularly, singularly, important to note (realize), for this reason, in fact, significant that, surprisingly
exception	aside from, barring, beside, except, excepting, excluding, exclusive of, other than, outside of, save
exemplifying	chiefly, especially, for instance, in particular, markedly, namely, particularly, including, specifically, such as, for example, in other words
generalizing	as a rule, as usual, for the most part, generally, generally speaking, ordinarily, usually
illustration	for example, for instance, for one thing, as an illustration, illustrated with, as an example, in this case
similarity	comparatively, coupled with, correspondingly, identically, likewise, similar, moreover, together with
restatement	in essence, in other words, namely, that is, that is to say, in short, in brief, to put it differently
sequence	at first, first of all, to begin with, in the first place, at the same time, for now, for the time being, the next step, in time, in turn, later on, meanwhile, next, then, soon, in the meantime, later, while, earlier, simultaneously, afterward, in conclusion, with this in mind
summarizing	after all, all in all, all things considered, briefly, by and large, in any case, in any event, in brief, in conclusion, on the whole, in short, in summary, in the final analysis, in the long run, on balance, to sum up, to summarize, finally

Dealing with Quotes

- **Use quotes to convince your reader of the validity of you analysis.** Don't use quotes that aren't meaningful or don't support your argument.

- **Provide the best possible quote to support your analysis.** A good rule for whether to use a quote or just paraphrase it is to ask yourself if the quote says something in a way that you could not say yourself.

  EX.: from *To Kill a Mockingbird*: **quote that could be paraphrased: [note: this takes place when a lynch mob comes to the jail where Atticus is protecting a prisoner.]** "'Go home, I [Atticus] said.' Jem shook his head. As Atticus's fists went to his hips, so did Jem's, and as they faced each other I could see little resemblance between them: Jem's soft brown hair and eyes, his oval face and snug-fitting ears were our mother's, contrasting oddly with Atticus's graying black hair and square-cut features, but they were somehow alike. Mutual defiance made them alike."

  paraphrased version: Jem's defiance of Atticus's order to go home and his decision to remain with his father to face the lynch mob shows that Jem is beginning to think for himself. The author further shows his maturity by pointing out the "mutual defiance" both he and his father display.

  quote that should be quoted: "'You never really understand a person until you consider things from his point of view --'" **[Look for quotes that point to the theme or define a character or illustrate the use of language.]**

- **Quote no more of the text than is necessary and relevant.**

  EX.: complete quote: "Jem gave a reasonable description of Boo: he was about six-and-a-half feet tall, judging by his tracks; he dined on raw squirrels and any cats he could catch, that's why his hands were bloodstained – if you ate an animal raw, you could never wash the blood off. There was a long jagged scar that ran across his face; what teeth he had were yellow and rotten; his eyes popped, and he drooled most of the time."

  pared down quote: Boo is described as a boogeyman with "eyes popped" and "yellow and rotten" teeth. He supposedly "dined on raw squirrels and any cats he could catch, that's why his hands were bloodstained."

- **If using a quote, quote the text exactly.** Punctuation and spelling within the quote should be exactly as in the original.

- **Every quote must be followed by a citation.** Use this format: "Neighbors bring food with death and flowers with sickness and little things in between," Scout recalls (p. 278).

- **Don't insert a quote without introducing it and then explaining** how it is support for the point you are making.

- **Don't use the word "quote" or "quotation,"** such as: This quote means.

- **When you're quoting what a character is saying, double quotation marks go on the outsi**de, indicating the passage is a quote, and single quotation marks go around what the character is saying. ex.: "Julie said, 'Hi,' to me." or "Julie said, 'Hi.'"

- **Quote lengthy passage rarely and only if every sentence in the passage is meaningful to your discussion.** (In a five-paragraph essay you would do this no more than once.) When quoting a passage that is three or more lines long, separate it from your own text and indent five more spaces. If you do this, you don't need to use quotation marks (unless someone is speaking within the quote.)

You *Do* Need to Proofread and Revise!

As painful as it may seem, what you have written so far if you have followed this guide is what is called a *first draft* – the word "first" meaning "being before all others," and the word "draft" meaning "subject to revision." A first draft is not a polished piece of writing. You need to go back through and check for things such as logical order, sentence structure, spelling, grammar, transitions, and cohesiveness.

 Take the time now to edit and revise.

Make sure you --

- ✓ Spellcheck your paper. However . . .

- ✓ Don't rely solely on spellcheck. It won't catch it if you use "their" instead of "there" or if you accidentally type "it" twice in a row.

- ✓ Use a grammar check. It will point out incorrect grammar or if you are using the passive voice. If you don't have a grammar check, I recommend that you install one on your computer. If you can't do that, you will have to read your paper silently with the purpose of finding and correcting any grammatical errors.

- ✓ Put your essay aside for a day. (Yes, this means you can't wait until the last minute to write it!)

- ✓ Look at your topic sentences. Do they support your thesis?

- ✓ Look at the sentences within each paragraph. Do they support the paragraph's topic sentence? If there is anything that doesn't, either delete it or move it to a paragraph where it does support the topic sentence.

- ✓ Look at your evidence. Does it support the supposition of the topic sentence?

- ✓ Look at your quotes. Is each of them meaningful? Get rid of the ones that aren't and find more meaningful quotes. Are they too long? If so, cut them down to their essence – the most important part of the quote. If they can be briefly paraphrased, do so. Do they have attribution? If not, properly indicate who said the quote. Are they quoted properly? Check for appropriate punctuation.

✓ Reread your paper out loud and listen for any awkward phrasings. Circle or underline wherever it doesn't read smoothly or the meaning isn't clear. Reread your paper silently to check for clear logic, unity, and smooth transitions. Correct any problem areas by rearranging and/or combining sentences and using a variety of sentence lengths and structures.

✓ When revising, vary length of sentences; most should be of medium length with some longer sentences and a very occasional short sentence (seven words or less). Use a short sentence for emphasis. Vary style of sentence. (Don't always follow a subject-verb pattern.)

✓ Reread your paper.

✓ Circle vague words, such as "bad" and "nice." Circle slang, such as "cool" and "bling" and informal language, such as "awesome" and "hang out." Use more precise and higher-level words.

✓ Circle all contractions that aren't contained within a quote. Change them to full words.

✓ Circle words that you repeat more than once and that seem too simplistic. Replace these with more sophisticated vocabulary.

✓ Use descriptive language.

✓ Change everything you've circled.

✓ Have someone else read your paper and make comments, especially pointing out where the meaning isn't clear.

What to Avoid . . .

Avoid beginning any sentence in a formal essay with the following. (This isn't a complete list!) Nearly all of these phrases are what I call "empty phrases." They add nothing. If you cut any of these off from the beginning of the sentence, you will see that your sentence has the same meaning. There's only one difference, the point of the sentence is now more directly stated and, thus, stronger and more effective.

In the novel (*not more than once*)	**Also**
This quote says	**In the book**
This is an example of	**But**
[character's name] says this on page x.	**Obviously**
The fact that	**There are**
In conclusion	**And**
This evidence explains	**Next**
So you can see by this that	**First**
This paragraph will explain	**Second**
It has been proven	**In my opinion**
By this (quote) I mean (it is meant)	**As you can see**
This next piece of evidence supports my thesis because	**I think that because**

Grammatical Rules to Remember

☐ Don't underline *your* title.

☐ Either underline or italicize the title of a book, play, or movie every time it's mentioned in your paper.

☐ Put double quotation marks around the titles of poems, short stories, and articles.

☐ Use parallel construction. **ex.: wrong:** Today during the Iron Man marathon, I am running five miles, swimming one mile, and will bike ten miles. **right:** Today during the Iron Man marathon, I am running five miles, swimming one mile, and biking ten miles.

☐ Make sure pronoun references agree in type and number. **ex.: wrong:** Everyone **(singular)** said they **(plural)** would come. **right:** Everyone said he or she would come; or, Those **(plural)** who were invited said they **(plural)** would come

☐ Make sure of subject-verb agreement. **ex. wrong:** The team **(subject, singular)** of boys are **(verb – predicate, plural)** on a winning streak. **right:** The team **(singular)** of boys is **(singular)** on a winning streak.

☐ Know the proper use of "their," "they're," and "there" and other homonyms.

☐ Numbers of one hundred and below are expressed in words; numbers above one hundred are expressed in numerals. Do not spell out numbers associated with ages or page numbers.

Essay Format

Copy both the Essay Template and the Outline Template to your files. Every time you use them, just do a save as and name the new file the name of your essay. You can do one of two things to begin your essay. 1.) Using the Outline Template, type in your sentences, then when you're done, delete all of the headings. This will give you almost a complete first draft. Go back and use the Essay Template to fill in and rewrite your essay. 2.) Use the Outline as your notes and use the Essay Template to type in your sentences below each label. When you're done, delete the labels.

Introduction

1. **Opener – an interesting introductory sentence:** Begin with something that will grab your reader's attention and make her want to read on.

2. **sentence that explains the opener:** Why did you choose the introductory sentence? Without explaining your thesis, explain what generally about this opener connects to your thesis.

3. **transition from the opener:** Tie your opener and explanation of it to the book and to the topic of the thesis

4. **sentences that discuss the topic of the thesis:** Connect the point of the first several sentences to the work you're writing about and then to your thesis.

5. **transition:** sentence that specifically transitions from the general topic of the thesis in the work to your thesis

6. **your thesis statement**

Body Paragraphs

1. **first sentence:** topic sentence that is the focus of the paragraph and that is something you need to prove in order to prove your thesis.

2. **bulk of the paragraph:** follow this pattern generally: *Make a point that will help prove your topic sentence – provide two pieces of evidence in the form of details, quotes, paraphrases – explanation as to how this evidence proves your point.* You can then do one of the following:

repeat the pattern if you have another, closely related point to make or provide more evidence for the first point.

3. **concluding sentence:** wrap up each paragraph by generally stating what you've proved in that paragraph in a way that relates it to the next paragraph.

Conclusion

1. **Restate your thesis:** Since you've proven your thesis in your essay, you can now consider it as if it is true.

2. **Discuss the deeper meaning:** Point out how your true thesis gives the reader a deeper understanding of the novel. Touch upon, but do not completely restate, the points you proved in your body paragraphs.

3. **Relate this meaning to something in the world:** How does this new understanding or appreciation of the novel help the reader to understand the world better? What should the reader learn or do as a result of discovering the truth of this thesis? You might want to refer to something you've mentioned in your Introduction, such as the ending of the anecdote you may have used or the repetition of a phrase or word.

4. **End with something interesting.** You might want to use a meaningful quote from the novel that movingly or shockingly expresses the main idea behind your paper; or with a thoughtful comment; or with a critical observation.

Essay Outline Template

Introduction:

- *[Type your grabber and next sentences that lead to the thesis statement here.]*

Thesis: (This is the last sentence of your Introduction. It is your main/controlling idea of the essay.)

- *[Type your thesis statement here.]*

Body Paragraph #1:

Topic sentence that introduces this paragraph and your first reason your thesis is correct. This is something you believe to be true that (if you prove it to be true) will, in part, prove your thesis statement.

- *[Type the topic sentence of your first body paragraph here.]*

Reason A why topic sentence #1 is true:

- *[Type your first reason why your topic sentence is true here.]*

Support for Reason A: (at least two strong facts, specific details, quotes, examples that prove or describe or otherwise support your reason.)

- *[Type support for Reason A, and then explain why this evidence is support for Reason A]*

Reason B why topic sentence #1 is true:

- *[Type your second reason why your topic sentence is true here.]*

Support for Reason B: (at least two strong facts, specific details, quotes, examples that prove or describe or otherwise support your reason.)

- *[Type support for Reason A, and then explain why this evidence is support for Reason A]*

  NOTE: Use this same Body Paragraph Outline Format for all of your Body Paragraphs.

Conclusion:

(Restate your thesis in a completely different way from how it appeared in your Introduction. State it as if it is now a proven fact that has meaning; sum up how the proof in your Body Paragraphs proves your thesis; explain why what the reader has learned in this essay is relevant to their lives; close essay with a strong statement.)

Shannon Michal Dow has Master degrees in Education and Remedial Reading and Remedial Language Arts and has taught English and literacy for a combined 10 years at the secondary level and as a college tutor to both undergraduate and graduate students. She earned an ETS Recognition of Excellence for her performance in English Language, Literature, and Composition: Content Knowledge PRAXIS II.

She also is a playwright and her plays and co-authored plays have been produced around the country and have received 19 awards and honors, including from the Julie Harris Playwright Competition, Beverly Hills Theatre Guild, L.A., CA; The Abingdon Theatre Company New Play Series, Off-Broadway, NYC; The Players Club, NY, NY; Writer's Digest Competition; Orlando Shakespeare New Plays Festival, FL; and the McLaren Memorial Comedy Competition, Midland, TX.

Her co-written play, *Killing Dante*, was published by Samuel French, Inc. in 2008, and her co-authored book, *Writing the Award Winning Play*, a beginner's and intermediate's guide to playwriting, was published in 2003.

She currently teaches English and literacy in Connecticut where she lives with her husband.

Phosphene Publishing Company publishes books and DVDs relating to literature, history, spirituality, education, the paranormal, film, Texana, and the martial arts.

For other great titles, visit

phosphenepublishing.com

Printed in Great Britain
by Amazon